# *Fast & Fabulous*
# Appetizers

## by Polly Clingerman

THE
AMERICAN
★ COOKING ★
GUILD™

Boynton Beach, Florida

**Dedication**
To Mom, who taught me that entertaining is fun. And to John, who tasted his way through the book with unflagging enthusiasm.

**Acknowledgments**
—Cover Design and Layout by Pearl & Associates, Inc.
—Cover Photo by Burwell and Burwell
—Edited by Marian Levine
—Typesetting & Layout by BOSS Services

**Revised Edition 1997**
Copyright © 1987 by Polly Clingerman
Formally published as *Fast & Fabulous Hors d' Oeuvres*
All rights reserved.
Printed in U.S.A.
ISBN 0-942320-27-1

**More...Quick Recipes for Creative Cooking!**
The American Cooking Guild's *Collector's Series* includes over 30 popular cooking topics such as Barbeque, Breakfast & Brunches, Chicken, Cookies, Hors d' Oeuvres, Seafood, Tea, Coffee, Pasta, Pizza, Salads, Italian and many more. Each book contains more than 50 selected recipes. For a catalog of these and many other full sized cookbooks, send $1 to the address below and a coupon will be included for $1 off your first order.

**Cookbooks Make Great Premiums!**
The American Cooking Guild has been the premier publisher of private label and custom cookbooks since 1981. Retailers, manufacturers, and food companies have all chosen The American Cooking Guild to publish their premium and promotional cookbooks. For further information on our special markets programs please contact the address.

**The American Cooking Guild**
3600-K South Congress Avenue
Boynton Beach, FL 33426

# Table of Contents

**Introduction** ...........................................................................5

**Hints for the Quick Cook** ..............................................6

**Hot Pickups**

Wonderful Onion Puffies ..........................................7

Plum Blossoms ...........................................................8

Olli's Tamales ............................................................9

Hot Chicken-Cheese Balls .......................................9

Meat Toasts ..............................................................10

Asparagus-Blue Cheese Rolls ...............................11

Pita Pizzas ................................................................12

Smoked Mussel Turnovers ....................................12

Shrimp Pillows ........................................................13

Things in Blankets ..................................................13

Crispy Tortilla Melts ..............................................14

Egg Benedict Bites ..................................................15

Melting Clam or Crab Mouthfuls ........................16

**Spear It!**

Mini Kabobs .............................................................17

Cocktail Franks in Peanut-Chutney Sauce .........18

Crispy Shrimp ..........................................................19

Bacon-Wrapped Morsels ........................................20

Tropical Sausage Medley .......................................23

Karen's Tuna Balls ..................................................24

Garlic Chicken Sticks ..............................................25

**For Forks Only**

Ellen's Broiled Oysters ..........................................26

Spicy Sausage Stroganoff ......................................27

Mozzarella-Anchovy Crostini ...............................28

Baked Garlic Oysters ..............................................29

**Hot Dips & A Spread**

Creamy Artichokes and Shrimp ...........................30

The Ultimate Crab Dip ..........................................31

Smoked Cheese and Wine Dip for Fruit .............32

Baked Almond Camembert ...................................33

Smoked Oyster Cheese Dip ...................................34

Southwestern Chili Dip ..........................................35

Cheesy Crab Dip ........................................................................35
Neapolitan Fondue ...................................................................36

## Cold Pickups
Turkey-Roquefort Rolls .............................................................37
Ham-Liverwurst Rolls................................................................38
Smoked Salmon-Asparagus Rolls .............................................39
Beef and Brie Croissants ..........................................................40
Daniel's Roquefort Endive .......................................................40
Shrimp Roquefort Splits ...........................................................41
Artichoke-Shrimp Canapés.......................................................41
Mimosa Shrimp .........................................................................42
Oriental Turkey or Chicken Cubes...........................................43
Sun-Dried Tomatoes, Basil and Cheese ...................................44
Roast Beef-Horseradish Roulades ...........................................45
Radish Canapés .........................................................................46
Doo Hickey (Radishes and Cheese) .........................................47
Ellen's Cucumber Sandwiches .................................................47
Pecan Mushrooms......................................................................48

## Cold Dips & Dunks
Louisiana Whipped Chili Dip....................................................49
Orange Mustard Dip..................................................................50
Snowy Chili Cheese Dip ...........................................................51
Pimento Dip ..............................................................................51
Jalapeño-Tuna Dip ....................................................................52
Curry Cream Dip.......................................................................52
Sesame Dip................................................................................53
Tostada Dip ...............................................................................54
Zucchini Rémoulade .................................................................55
Sue's Spinach Dip .....................................................................56
Judy's Hummos..........................................................................57
Layered Caviar Dip ...................................................................58

## Cold Spreads
Strawberry Cheese-Nut Ring.....................................................59
Two Minute Elegant Pâté ..........................................................60
Caviar Quickie...........................................................................60
Shrimp Curry Spread.................................................................61
Brie and Butter Mosaic .............................................................61
Liverwurst Pâté .........................................................................62
Crab Alaska................................................................................63
Lightning Alaska .......................................................................63
Madras Chicken Bites ...............................................................64

# Introduction

This book was born when a busy friend asked me to recommend a book of appetizer recipes that could be made in ten minutes. "There has to be something beyond onion soup dip!"

"I must have a hundred recipes," I said. And it turned out I did: wonderful morsels that take little time and don't have "hurry" written all over them – gourmet appetizers to serve after-work guests while they watch you make dinner; scrumptious noshes to make quickly when you volunteer the appetizers for a friend's party; elegant tidbits to accompany pre-theater drinks. With the recipes in this book you can impress the guests you invited or the friends who pop in unexpectedly.

Everyone who heard of my project was enthusiastic. And so, here is *Fast & Fabulous Appetizers* – gourmet recipes for people who have more social urge than time. The recipes can be prepared in 10 to 20 minutes. unless you are preparing large quantities. When you are pressed for time and have more than 6 or 8 guests, go heavy on dips and dunks and spreads and light on individual items. Another time comment: many recipes require little work by you since their preparation time is all in the oven. Always start them first so you can use that oven time for other things.

This book is filled with yummy tastes: hot and cold dunks and spreads; a luscious, cheesy crab dip; crispy bacon-wrapped morsels; golden, biscuit-covered sausages. Try the shrimp sandwich with Roquefort cheese or the implausible and fabulous smoked oyster-cheese dip that makes itself in minutes and is pure heaven. I tried to include a good mix of familiar and unfamiliar recipes. My rule of thumb in selecting them was, if you don't automatically reach for a second, it doesn't go in. As you cook your way through the book, I think you'll agree that this is all real second (and third) helping stuff. Bon Appetit!

# Hints for the Quick Cook

◆ Watch for the substitutions in the ingredients lists. Often, we suggest a substitution to make preparation even speedier.

◆ Keep recipe-ready ingredients in the refrigerator and freezer. Freeze chopped and grated ingredients in flat packages (no more than ½ to ¾ inch thick) so you can easily break off what you need while still frozen.

◆ When you buy cheese, grate and package it immediately. If you will use it within a week, leave it in the refrigerator; if not, freeze it.

◆ Keep a jar of grated Parmesan cheese in the freezer. Grate this yourself from a good, fresh block — don't use the cardboard-tube stuff that tastes like its container.

◆ Chop onions and freeze them in a flat package.

◆ Chop parsley and keep some in the refrigerator for garnish, some in the freezer for an ingredient. (Thawed parsley tastes fine but is too limp for garnishing.)

◆ Grate a bunch of soft bread crumbs and freeze.

◆ Partially fry bacon, freeze the strips separately on a baking sheet and package them. It speeds future cooking, and eliminates a step when preparing bacon-wrapped foods.

◆ Once opened, freeze tomato paste in teaspoon-size portions on a baking sheet, then package. (Opened tomato paste doesn't keep long in the refrigerator.)

◆ Cook a whole chicken, cut the meat into bite-size pieces and freeze in 1 or 2-cup amounts. Remember too, you can always buy cooked chickens at a deli counter.

---

**The Quick Cook** 🕐

If you are in a tearing rush, or if your guests are getting grumpy and you must feed them immediately, head for the recipes marked with a clock. These are super quick; so quick, in fact, that you can practically start them when you hear the car door slam and be finished in time to answer the bell.

---

# Hot Pickups

◆

## Wonderful Onion Puffies

I added the "wonderful" in case you said "Ho hum, onions," and started to flip the page. These have saved me countless times when guests dropped in unannounced and I wanted to serve something good without missing the conversation.

  $^1/_4$   cup grated Parmesan cheese
  $^1/_4$   cup mayonnaise
2 to 3   small yellow onions (about 2 inches in diameter)
5 to 7   slices of firm, closed-textured white bread

Mix cheese and mayonnaise in a small bowl. Slice the onions paper thin. Cut the bread into 20 rounds, about 2 inches in diameter. On each bread round place a complete onion slice. The slice should be the same diameter as the bread. Top with a generous teaspoon of cheese mixture. Place the rounds on a baking sheet and run under the broiler for 2 to 3 minutes, or until puffed and golden. Watch carefully because they brown quickly.

Transfer onto a pretty serving platter and serve hot.

**Yield:** 20 pieces

---

The Quick Cook 🕐
Closed-textured bread is the firm, homemade style loaf of bread like those made by Pepperidge Farm® or Arnold®.

# Plum Blossoms

Elegant hot little puffs of crab with an elusive Oriental flavor. You'll find duck sauce or plum sauce in the international section of your grocery store.

4   *slices close-texture white bread*
1   *cup fresh crab meat, well picked over for cartilage*
2   *Tablespoons water chestnuts, chopped fine*
1   *Tablespoon soy sauce*
1   *slice fresh ginger root (size of a nickel), chopped fine*
1/2  *teaspoon sesame oil*
1   *Tablespoon duck sauce (sometimes called plum sauce)*
1   *teaspoon brown sugar*
    *salt, to taste*
1/2  *cup mayonnaise, divided*

Remove crusts from bread, toast lightly and cut each slice into 6 pieces. (Cut 3 strips, then halve each across the middle.)

In a small bowl mix crab, water chestnuts, soy sauce, ginger root, sesame oil, duck sauce, brown sugar, salt and about ¼ cup mayonnaise, enough to hold mixture together nicely. Heap crab mixture on toast squares, covering surface completely so the toast edges won't burn. Spread the top of each with a thin layer of mayonnaise.

Place the canapés on a baking sheet and run them under the broiler, 4 to 5 inches from the heat, until bubbly and golden. This takes only a minute, so don't leave them. Transfer to a platter and serve hot.

**Yield:** 24

---

**The Quick Cook** 🕐
When in a hurry, I leave the bread whole, top it with crab mixture, broil and then cut into pieces. To save time, use a 7-ounce can of crab meat and ½ teaspoon powdered ginger for the fresh ginger root.

# Olli's Tamales

I'm grateful that Olli thought up these crispy bacon-wrapped bites.

  1   *14-ounce can tamales, hot or mild*
 12  *slices bacon*

Preheat oven to 500°. Unwrap tamales and cut each into 4 pieces. In a large skillet fry bacon for 3 minutes to render out some of the fat. Wrap each tamale piece in half a slice of bacon. Place on a rack over a shallow pan and bake at 500° for about 10 minutes or until the bacon is crisp. Serve hot on a doily lined plate. Provide plenty of napkins.

**Yield:** 24

---

# Hot Chicken-Cheese Balls

Hot and cheesy — wonderful little mouthfuls.

  1  *cup cooked chicken, shredded or chopped fine*
$1/3$  *cup shredded Gruyère cheese*
$1/4$  *cup finely chopped celery*
  3  *Tablespoons mayonnaise*
  1  *Tablespoon chopped parsley*
$1/8$  *teaspoon hot pepper sauce, or to taste*
$1/4$  *teaspoon dried tarragon*
     *salt and pepper, to taste*

Preheat oven to 350°.

In a small bowl combine all ingredients. If you have time, chill for five minutes in the freezer to make mixture easier to handle. Roll mixture into one-inch balls and place them on a lightly greased baking sheet. Bake at 350° for 8 minutes or until lightly browned. Serve hot.

**Yield:** about 30

---

**The Quick Cook** ⏰
To save time, substitute a 6½-ounce can cooked chicken for the chopped chicken.

# Meat Toasts

Eat these hearty little toasts hot out of the oven.

    1   *pound ground beef*
    1   *medium onion, minced*
    1   *teaspoon salt*
  1/2  *teaspoon black pepper*
    1   *Tablespoon horeseradish*
  10  *slices firm, close-textured white bread*
        *soft butter, as needed*
        *prepared mustard, as needed*

Mix ground beef, onion, salt, pepper and horseradish.

Butter one side of each bread slice and place on baking sheet, butter side down. Spread the unbuttered side with mustard. Pat about 1/4 cup of meat mixture on the mustard side, spreading it to the edges.

Using a serrated bread knife, cut the crusts off the bread, angling the knife so no bare bread is left exposed (anything that sticks out can burn and taste bitter). Cut each into 4 squares, and broil 5 to 6 inches from the heat for 3 to 4 minutes, or until lightly browned and a bit crusty.

Transfer to a platter and serve hot.

**Variation:** Substitute 1/2 teaspoon of your favorite herb for the horseradish.

**Yield:** 40

---

**Quick Tip**

When you broil or bake things on toast or tortilla rounds, you must completely cover the toast or tortilla with filling. Any exposed area will burn before the topping has puffed and browned.

# Asparagus-Blue Cheese Rolls

These are heavenly. Use the soft, floppy white bread that kids love.

   *12*   *slices soft white bread, crusts removed*
   *1/3*   *cup blue cheese, at room temperature*
          *mayonnaise, to taste*
   *12*   *cooked asparagus spears, very well drained*
*1/3 to 1/2*   *cup melted butter*

Preheat oven to 375°.

Using a rolling pin, gently flatten each slice of bread to about half the original thickness. In a small bowl mix blue cheese with enough mayonnaise to make it spreadable. Spread each slice with a generous teaspoon of the cheese mixture. Place an asparagus spear on one end of the bread and roll it up. (Spears should be cut to the length of the bread, but if they're a little longer, it's all right.)

Melt butter in a small skillet. Dip each roll in melted butter to coat all surfaces. Place seam-down on a cookie sheet. Bake at 375° for 10 to 12 minutes or until crisp and brown. Cut each roll into 4 pieces.

**Note:** Asparagus spears should not be too thin, 3/8 to 1/2-inch in diameter is about right.

**Yield:** 48

# Pita Pizzas

Quick, crisp-crusted and good!

      3   pita breads (5-inch size)
      1   14-ounce jar pizza sauce
     48   slices pepperoni
  2 to 3  cups mozzarella cheese, grated

Preheat the broiler.

Split each pita in half to make 6 thin rounds, then quarter each round. Spread each wedge with about 1 tablespoon of sauce, spreading it to the edges (any exposed edge will burn). Top each with 2 slices pepperoni, then 1 to 2 tablespoons cheese.

Broil 5 inches from the heat until the cheese melts. Watch very carefully — it takes only a minute or so. Transfer to a platter and serve hot.

**Yield:** 24 wedges

---

# Smoked Mussel Turnovers

Melting, fried turnovers with wonderful centers! Made with the prepared pie crust from the supermarket dairy case, they take almost no time. Serve them plain or, the way we like them, with a bowl of good tartar sauce.

          oil for deep frying
      3   cans (3¹/₂ to 4 ounces each) smoked mussels
      1   15-ounce package ready-to-use pie crusts

Start heating 2 inches of oil in a pan for deep frying.

Drain mussels. Cut pie crust into 2-inch rounds. Put a mussel on one side of each round. Wet the rim of each circle with a dampened finger, fold over and pinch edges to seal.

Fry in 350° oil for 1 to 3 minutes, just until golden, watching carefully.

**Yield:** about 60

# Shrimp Pillows

Yummy shrimp coated with mayonnaise and baked in flaky, golden pastry. The mayonnaise gives the turnovers a wonderful texture.

> 1  15-ounce package ready-to-use pie crusts
> 20 medium-size shrimp, cooked, shelled and deveined
> $3/4$ cup mayonnaise, or more to taste
> lemon pepper, to taste

Preheat oven to 450°.

Cut 3-inch circles of pie crust. Dip each shrimp into mayonnaise, coating it generously (or spread the mayonnaise on all sides). Lay a shrimp on one side of each dough circle. Sprinkle with lemon pepper. Fold dough over and pinch the edges to seal well.

Bake at 450° for 8 to 10 minutes or until golden.

Transfer to platter and serve hot.

**Yield:** 20

---

# Things in Blankets

Watch your guests' faces when they see a platter of these golden, dough-wrapped morsels.

> 1  10-ounce tube refrigerated biscuits
> 40 pieces total of any of the following: green or black pitted olives, 1-inch sticks of salami or pepperoni, $1/2$-inch cubes of cheese, drained and rinsed anchovies or cocktail sausages
> 1  cup grated Parmesan cheese, approximately

Preheat oven to 375°.

Cut each biscuit in quarters, stretch the dough into a small rope, and wrap it around the center of each item. Wrap long items like cocktail sausages or salami sticks just around their middles. Roll each in parmesan cheese. Place on greased baking sheet and bake at 375° for 6 to 8 minutes or until golden. Transfer to paper doily lined platter and serve hot.

**Yield:** 40

# Crispy Tortilla Melts

Gooey, crispy and fired up with chilies. No one leaves this platter alone until it is empty.

|  | oil for frying |
|---|---|
| 4 | flour tortillas, 8-inch diameter |
| 1/8 to 1/4 | teaspoon salt |
| 1 | cup Monterey Jack cheese, grated |
| 2/3 | cup Cheddar cheese, grated |
| 1/2 | cup chopped, canned green chilies, drained |
| 2/3 | cup chopped onion |

Preheat oven to 375°.

Heat 1/4-inch of oil in a 9 or 10-inch skillet to 350°. Fry tortillas quickly (30 to 60 seconds per side) until pale gold. Prick puffed spots with a fork as they fry to keep them as flat as possible. Drain on paper towels. Sprinkle with salt.

Place two tortillas on a cookie sheet. Sprinkle each with half of each cheese, half the chilies and half the onions, covering the entire surface. Top with the remaining tortillas and press down lightly.

Bake at 375° for 8 to 10 minutes or until the cheese begins to ooze and is melted and gooey. Watch carefully as you approach the 8 minute mark. Remove from oven, cut in wedges; 6 or 8 per round.

Serve immediately while still crispy and hot. Provide plenty of napkins.

**Yield:** 12 to 16 wedges

# Egg Benedict Bites

Wonderful little mouthfuls with all the smoky, buttery richness of their big brothers. Don't blanch at the thought of making Hollandaise Sauce. Done in a blender or food processor, it takes less than five minutes.

　　　　3　egg yolks
　　　　2　Tablespoons lemon juice
　　　1/4　teaspoon salt
　　　　　　pinch pepper
　　　1/2　cup melted butter
　8 to 12　slices close-textured white bread
　　　　6　slices cooked ham, 1/8-inch thick
　　　　6　hard-cooked eggs (24 nice center slices)

In the container of a food processor or blender, place egg yolks, lemon juice, salt and pepper. Process for 5 seconds. With the motor running, pour in the melted butter, leaving the milky residue from the butter behind in the pan. The Hollandaise Sauce will thicken almost immediately; turn off motor and set sauce aside.

Preheat broiler.

Toast the bread, then cut it into 24 2-inch rounds and place them on a baking sheet. Cut ham in 2-inch rounds. Slice eggs (an egg slicer makes this a lot easier). On each toast place a piece of ham and an egg slice. Top with Hollandaise sauce, making sure to cover the egg completely so it doesn't dry out.

Run under the broiler about 3 inches from the heat for 1 to 2 minutes — just enough to heat the sauce and brown it delicately. Serve hot on a pretty plate.

**Yield:** 24

# Melting Clam or Crab Mouthfuls

Use either crab or clams. The clams are faster (you don't have to pick them over for cartilage) and a lot cheaper. On the other hand, crab is delicious! Both are guaranteed to enchant your guests in these wonderful, oozy, cheesy bites.

    1  *can (7 ounces) clams or crab, drained\**
    1  *Tablespoon minced onion*
    1  *cup grated Swiss cheese*
  *1/2*  *cup mayonnaise*
    1  *teaspoon fresh lemon juice*
  *1/8*  *teaspoon thyme or basil*
    1  *package (8 rolls) crescent refrigerator rolls*
    1  *can (5 ounces) water chestnuts*

Preheat oven to 375°.

In a medium bowl combine clams or crabs, onion, cheese, mayonnaise, lemon juice and thyme or basil. Mix well.

Unroll the dough and gently press out the diagonal dividing lines (you'll be left with 4 large rectangles). Cut each rectangle in half lengthwise and in thirds widthwise, resulting in 6 squares per rectangle. Place them, not touching, on an ungreased baking sheet. Heap some cheese mixture on each. Top each with a few slices of water chestnuts. Bake at 375° for 10 to 12 minutes.

Serve hot on a doily lined plate.

**Yield:** 24

\*If using crab meat, pick it over carefully for cartiledge.

# Spear It!

## Mini Kabobs

Tiny skewers of oysters, shrimp and bacon, nipped up with a cocktail onion.

24   *small raw oysters*
24   *1-inch bacon squares*
24   *medium raw shrimp, shelled and deveined*
24   *pickled onions*
24   *toothpicks for skewering*

On each toothpick place an oyster, a bacon square, a shrimp and a pickled onion. The items should be roughly the same size so the skewer cooks evenly. If the oysters are small, fold the bacon square in quarters to make a fat little cube and cut the shrimp in half. Use your judgement; just try for uniform size.

Broil skewers 6 inches from the heat for 3 to 4 minutes. Turn and broil 1 to 2 minutes more. Or, bake on a rack over a shallow pan at 400° for 10 to 12 minutes until the bacon is cooked and kabobs are slightly golden. Transfer to a platter and serve hot.

**Yield:** 24

# Cocktail Franks in Peanut-Chutney Sauce

A creamy Oriental mix of peanut butter spiked with chutney bathing cocktail-size frankfurters. This is also a delicious dip for chicken nuggets, fried chicken wings or whatever. Be creative. It's wonderful.

*1/2  cup smooth peanut butter*
*1/4  cup Major Grey's mango chutney*
*1  cup chicken stock*
*2  Tablespoons white corn syrup*
*1  clove garlic, crushed*
*1  pound cocktail-size frankfurters*

In a saucepan, combine the peanut butter, chutney, chicken stock, corn syrup and garlic. Cook gently, stirring often, until the sauce is thick and smooth, about 4 minutes. Add frankfurters and cook until they are well heated and nicely coated with the sauce, about 5 minutes more.

Serve in a chafing dish or a shallow heatproof bowl set on a warmer. Provide cocktail picks for spearing.

**Note:** If you can't find cocktail-size frankfurters, substitute regular size frankfurters cut into 1-inch pieces.

**Yield:** about 40

# Crispy Shrimp

A really quick recipe that people adore. Make more than you planned to make, because people will eat more than they planned to eat. My husband is addicted to these shrimp unadorned, but for opulent moments when you feel constrained to gild the lily, serve them with the Orange Mustard Dip on page 50.

> 1 package (10 ounces) frozen cooked shrimp
> 1 cup flour, approximately
>    oil for frying
>    Orange-Mustard Dip, page 50

Thaw shrimp as directed on package and dry thoroughly on paper towels. Put flour on a piece of wax paper.

Heat a large skillet and add enough oil to film it by about ⅛-inch.

Toss shrimp with flour. Shake off any excess. When the oil reaches 350° begin frying the shrimp in small batches so they never crowd the skillet. Keep tossing the shrimp over high heat until golden and crispy, about 1 minute. Turn out onto paper towels to drain. Heap onto a warm serving plate and serve immediately with toothpicks for spearing.

Serve plain or with the Orange-Mustard Dip, page 50.

**Note:** The shrimp I like for this are labeled "large" but when they come out of the package they are curled up to a size a little bigger than a nickel — not what I would call large, but perfect for this recipe.

**Yield:** 6 servings, if guests aren't greedy as some of my friends

# Bacon-Wrapped Morsels

Crispy bacon-wrapped tidbits are perennial favorites. I have yet to encounter a guest whose eyes don't light up at the sight of them. Make an assortment and you'll have a hit on your hands. I give you some general instructions and follow with specific recipes telling how to handle the basic ingredients, ending with "proceed as in basic recipe." Read the basic instructions carefully, then choose your items to be wrapped and take off.

# Basic Recipe
> *bacon slices*
> *chosen ingredients to be wrapped (suggestions follow in the next five recipes)*

Prepare the item to be wrapped as instructed in each recipe.

Precook the bacon by frying it for 2 to 3 minutes to render out some of the fat. This way the morsel will brown and crisp up more quickly. Most items will require about a half slice of bacon. Wrap the morsel, secure it with a toothpick, place on a rack and cook one of two ways:

(1) Broil 5 to 6 inches from the heat for 3 to 4 minutes, turn and broil 1 to 2 minutes more, or until bacon is crisp.

(2) Bake in a preheated oven at 400° for 12 to 15 minutes or until bacon is crisp.

# Shrimpies

Shrimp broiled in a crisp bacon jacket are delicious. Consider serving them with the Orange Mustard Dipping Sauce on page 50.

> 24  *large raw shrimp, shelled and deveined*
> 12  *slices bacon, halved*

Pat shrimp dry. Proceed as in the Basic Recipe, above. Serve hot on a doily lined platter.

**Yield:** 24

# Angels on Horseback

A classic combination that always delights, though what on earth it has to do with angels or horses is a puzzlement. Big oysters are dreadful for this. No matter how long they broil, they emerge wet and disagreeable and give a bad name to oysters, angels and horsebacks. Avoid them.

24 *medium oysters or 2 cans oysters (8 ounces each), drained*
*black pepper, to taste*
12 *slices bacon, halved*

Drain oysters well and pat dry. Shake on a little black pepper. Continue as in Basic Recipe (page 20). Serve hot.

**Yield:** 24

# Peanut Prunes

Bacon and prunes make a great combination. If you have time, soak the prunes in gin for 30 minutes (or overnight). Drain well before proceeding.

18 *medium to large prunes, pitted*
6 *Tablespoons crunchy peanut butter*
9 *strips bacon, halved*

Put about 1 teaspoon peanut butter in each prune; the amount will vary, of course, with the size of the prune.

Continue as in Basic Recipe (page 20) using half a strip of bacon for each. Serve hot.

**Yield:** 18

# Bombay Babies

This time the prunes are stuffed with chutney. Delicious.

    18   medium to large prunes, pitted
     3   Tablespoons Major Grey's mango chutney
     9   slices bacon, halved

Stuff each prune with a teaspoon of chutney. Proceed as in Basic Recipe (page 20). Serve hot.

**Yield:** 18

# Cupid's Darts

Almonds and bacon adorning artichoke hearts may be aphrodisiac as the name suggests, maybe not. You might just try them and see.

        1   can (8 ounces) artichoke hearts in water
    2 to 3   Tablespoons slivered almonds
       16   slices bacon (approximately), halved

Drain artichokes well. Quarter each and tuck a few slivered almonds between the leaves. Proceed as in Basic Recipe (page 20).

**Yield:** about 30 to 32

# Tropical Sausage Medley

A tempting mix of little wieners and smoked sausages in a spicy orange sauce.

   1  *cup sugar*
   2  *Tablespoons cornstarch*
   8  *whole cloves*
  1/4  *teaspoon cinnamon*
1 1/2  *cups orange juice*
  1/4  *cup white vinegar*
 10  *ounces cocktail-size smoked sausages*
 10  *ounces cocktail-size wieners*

In a wide-bottomed pan mix sugar, cornstarch, cloves and cinnamon. Add orange juice and vinegar. Cook over medium heat, stirring constantly until thick. Add sausages and wieners and cook slowly for about five minutes, or until well heated.

Serve in a pretty heatproof dish over a warmer or in a chafing dish over low heat. Provide cocktail picks for spearing.

**Yield:** about 60 pieces

---

Quick Tip
Rub toothpicks with a cut clove of garlic and use them to spear cheese, meat or seafood. The garlic will add a subtle taste.

# Karen's Tuna Balls

I tasted this at a morning coffee, loved it, got the recipe and produced an absolute pasty horror because I made it in my new food processor. So a word of caution. Use the processor to make the bread crumbs, chop the almonds, onions and parsley, but unless you have a hair-trigger touch, combine this mixture by hand.

>     1    can tuna (7 ounces), drained
>    1/2   cup soft bread crumbs
>     2    Tablespoons chopped almonds
>     2    Tablespoons chopped parsley
>     2    Tablespoons chopped onion
>     1    egg
>     3    Tablespoons mayonnaise
>     1    teaspoon Dijon mustard
>    1/2   teaspoon poultry seasoning
>    1/2   cup melted butter
>    1/2   cup cornflake crumbs

Preheat oven to 400°.

Flake tuna and combine with bread crumbs, almonds, parsley, onion, egg, mayonnaise, mustard and poultry seasoning. Put the melted butter in a saucer and the crumbs on a piece of wax paper. Form the mixture into 1-inch balls and roll them first in crumbs, then butter. Place them on a baking sheet and bake at 400° for 10 minutes. Transfer to a platter and serve hot; provide toothpicks for spearing.

**Yield:** 35 to 40

---

### The Quick Cook ⏰
To save time, buy pre-chopped almonds, substitute frozen chopped onions for the fresh chopped onion, and buy packaged crumbs instead of making your own.

---

# Garlic Chicken Sticks

Wonderful garlicky, mini-skewers of chicken to dip in garlic butter.

*½   cup butter, at room temperature*
*1   green onion, minced*
*1   teaspoon crushed garlic*
*1   teaspoon lemon juice*
*1   teaspoon oregano*
*¼   teaspoon freshly ground pepper*
*¼   teaspoon paprika*
*     pinch salt*
*1   whole chicken breast, boned and skinned (8 ounces)*
*     salt and pepper, to taste*
*     toothpicks for skewering*

Preheat broiler.

Melt butter in a small saucepan. Add green onion, garlic, lemon juice, oregano, pepper, paprika and salt. Set aside.

Cut chicken into ½-inch cubes. Shake a little salt and pepper over the cubes and toss to coat lightly. Thread 3 or 4 cubes on each toothpick. Roll the chicken sticks in garlic butter, coating them well. Broil 4 inches from the heat for 5 minutes, turn and broil 5 minutes more.

Heat the remaining garlic butter and pour it into a small serving dish. Transfer the chicken sticks to a platter and serve hot with garlic butter for dipping. Provide plenty of napkins.

Note: If time allows, let the coated chicken stand about 30 minutes before broiling to allow flavors to penetrate.

**Yield:** 8 to 10 servings, about 20 sticks

# For Forks Only

◆

## Ellen's Broiled Oysters

Ellen is one of the best cooks I know. Her "dump and pour" style produces culinary delights but drives recipe writers nuts. Here is her way with oysters, in recipe-book measures.

| | |
|---|---|
| 1/4 | cup chili sauce |
| 1 | teaspoon bottled horseradish |
| 1 | Tablespoon seasoned dry bread crumbs |
| 1 | pint small to medium oysters, well drained |
| 2 | Tablespoons minced onion |
| 6 to 8 | slices bacon, cut in 1-inch squares |

In a small bowl mix chili sauce, horseradish and bread crumbs.

Place oysters in a shallow pan or dish that can go under the broiler. Put a little onion on each oyster , then a little of the sauce mixture. Top with a bacon square and run them under the broiler, about 4 inches from the heat, until the bacon is crisp; 4 to 5 minutes. Watch them carefully. Serve hot and provide small plates and forks.

Note: Big oysters are dreadful for this. No matter how long they broil, they emerge wet and disagreeable.

**Yield:** 4 to 6 servings

# Spicy Sausage Stroganoff

This is a natural for a New Year's buffet or to accompany the rehash of the last football game.

|     |     |
| --- | --- |
| 1 | clove garlic, halved |
| 2 | pounds fresh pork sausage, mild or hot |
| 1/4 | cup flour |
| 2 | cups water |
| 2 | chicken bouillon cubes |
| 2 | medium onions, chopped |
| 1 1/2 | cups fresh mushrooms, sliced |
| 1/4 | cup butter |
| 2 | teaspoons soy sauce |
| 2 | Tablespoons Worcestershire sauce |
| 1 | teaspoon dry mustard |
| 1 | teaspoon tomato paste |
| 1/4 | teaspoon liquid hot pepper sauce, optional |
| 2 | cups sour cream |

Rub a large, cold skillet with the garlic. Heat the skillet, add sausage, and brown it quickly on medium high heat, using a wooden spoon to crumble it as much as possible. Stir flour into the sausage and add water and bouillon cubes. Simmer 3 to 4 minutes, or until the mixture thickens slightly. Set aside.

In another skillet sauté onions and mushrooms in butter over medium heat for 4 to 5 minutes, or until softened, stirring constantly. Add them to the sausage mixture along with soy sauce, Worcestershire sauce, mustard, tomato paste and hot pepper sauce. (If you are using hot sausage, you may not want to add hot pepper sauce.) Heat thoroughly until the mixture bubbles. Remove from heat and stir in the sour cream. Pour the stroganoff into a chafing dish or a heatproof bowl that can be placed on a warmer. Serve with slices of warm, crusty French bread.

**Yield:** 6 cups, enough for 12 servings

---

**The Quick Cook** ⏰
Substitute frozen chopped onion for the fresh onion. Use 1 can (8 ounces) sliced mushrooms, drained, for the fresh. This dish freezes well. If you make it ahead for freezing, don't add sour cream until you reheat.

---

# Mozzarella-Anchovy Crostini

Crispy little fried cheese sandwiches drizzled with anchovy butter.

| | |
|---|---|
| 1/2 | cup unsalted butter |
| 4 | anchovy fillets, finely chopped |
| 2 | teaspoons drained capers, minced |
| 2 | teaspoons lemon juice |
| 1 | Tablespoon parsley, minced |
| 16 | thin slices firm-textured white bread |
| 8 | slices (1-ounce each) mozzarella, or any mild cheese |
| 2 | eggs, lightly beaten |
| 2 | Tablespoons milk |
| 4 to 6 | Tablespoons vegetable oil, for frying |
| 4 to 6 | Tablespoons unsalted butter, for frying |

To make anchovy butter sauce, melt 1/2 cup butter in a small saucepan. Add anchovies, capers, lemon juice and parsley. Taste and add a little more lemon if it needs perking up. Set aside.

Cut crust off the bread slices. Make 8 sandwiches, using one slice of cheese in each sandwich. Trim the cheese so it is a little smaller than the bread, leaving a 1/4-inch margin of bread.

In a flat dish or deep plate, mix egg and milk. Dip sandwich into egg mixture, coating on both sides.

In a large skillet heat 2 tablespoons each of oil and butter over medium to high heat. Fry sandwiches for one minute on each side, or until golden. (Lower the heat if they start to burn.) Remove cooked sandwiches to a paper towel and continue to fry sandwiches, adding more oil and butter as needed. Cut each sandwich into four pieces and place on a warm platter. If you won't serve them immediately, keep warm in a 200° oven. Reheat the anchovy sauce, if necessary, and drizzle over the sandwiches just before serving.

These can be eaten with the fingers if you provide plenty of napkins, but maybe it is kindest to provide small forks and plates.

**Yield:** 32

# Baked Garlic Oysters

Buttery, garlicky oysters with a hint of cheese. A wonderful fork hors d'oeuvre to serve with dry white wine on a chilly evening.

$^1/_2$   cup butter, divided
$1^1/_2$   cups soft bread crumbs (about 3 to 4 slices of bread)
$1^1/_2$   teaspoons finely chopped garlic
$^1/_4$   cup minced parsley
48   small to medium oysters
$^1/_3$   cup Parmesan cheese, grated

In a medium skillet, melt $^1/_4$ cup of butter. Add the bread crumbs and garlic and toss over medium heat for 2 or 3 minutes until crumbs are crisp and golden. Add the parsley.

In a greased, shallow ovenproof dish, spread two-thirds of the bread crumb mixture and lay the oysters on the crumbs. Mix cheese with the remaining crumbs and pat the mixture over the oysters. Dot with the second $^1/_4$ cup butter (use little $^1/_8$-inch bits).

Bake on the top shelf of a 400° oven for 10 minutes or until the crumbs are golden, the juices are bubbling and all is well heated. Put dish on warmer and serve immediately. Provide little plates and forks for this, and prepare to run out, no matter how many you have fixed.

**Yield:** 8 servings

# Hot Dips &
# A Spread

◆

## Creamy Artichokes and Shrimp

A luxurious, hot, seductive dish to serve when you want to spoil your guests just a little.

  8   *ounces cooked shrimp, peeled and deveined*
  1   *can (13 ounces) artichoke hearts, drained*
  1   *cup mayonnaise*
  1   *cup grated Parmesan cheese*
 ¹/₄  *teaspoon freshly ground pepper*
      *salt, to taste*
 ¹/₈  *teaspoon grated lemon rind*
  2   *drops hot sauce*

Preheat oven to 400°.

Finely chop shrimp and artichoke hearts. In a medium bowl combine them with the mayonnaise, Parmesan cheese, pepper, salt, lemon rind and hot sauce. Pour into a shallow 1-quart baking dish such as a 9-inch oven-proof glass pie plate. Bake at 400° for 10 minutes, or until the mixture is heated through and bubbly.

Serve hot, either in a chafing dish or over a warmer with crusty French bread, melba toast or whole wheat crackers.

**Yield:** about 4 cups

# The Ultimate Crab Dip

You may be proud of your crab dip, but wait until you taste this fabulous concoction.

  2  *shallots, minced (or the white part of 2 green onions)*
  1  *clove garlic, minced*
  $^1/_2$  *cup butter*
  $^1/_4$  *cup dry sherry*
  1  *pound fresh crab, well picked over for cartilage*
  $^1/_4$  *cup mayonnaise*
  $^1/_2$  *cup whipping cream*
  1  *package (3 ounces) plain or herb-flavored cream cheese*
  $^1/_4$  *teaspoon nutmeg*
    *grated rind of 1 lemon*
    *few drops hot pepper sauce*
  $^1/_4$  *teaspoon salt, or more to taste*
    *few grinds black pepper*

In a medium-size heavy saucepan, sauté shallots and garlic in butter over medium heat for 5 minutes. Add sherry, raise heat to high and cook 2 minutes more. Add crab, mayonnaise, whipping cream and cream cheese (cut into small chunks before adding). Reduce heat to medium-low and stir gently until well heated but not boiling. Add nutmeg, lemon rind, hot pepper sauce and salt and pepper to taste.

Serve hot in a chafing dish or over a warmer. The heat should be gentle so the sauce never simmers. Serve with warmed, crusty French bread or the best melba toast you can find.

**Yield:** 4 cups

# Smoked Cheese and Wine Dip for Fruit

Something a bit different. Serve this smoky, wine-tinged fondue with wedges of apple and pear. It's also a marvelous fondue dip for chips, French bread or cocktail franks.

2 Tablespoons butter
2 Tablespoons flour
2 cups half and half
1 teaspoon Dijon mustard
3 cups shredded smoked Cheddar or Gouda cheese
1/4 teaspoon nutmeg
1/3 cup dry white wine
1 Tablespoon brandy

In a medium-size saucepan over medium heat, melt the butter, then stir in flour and cook for one minute. Gradually stir in the half and half and the mustard, and cook and stir until thickened. Slowly add cheese. Continue to cook over low heat, stirring, until cheese has melted. Blend in nutmeg, wine and brandy. Pour mixture into a chafing dish or a serving dish that can sit over a warmer.

Accompany with wedges of apples and pears and some chunks of French bread. Remember to stir the sauce from time to time. It will thicken as it sits, so thin with a little milk if necessary.

**Yield:** 12 servings

# Baked Almond Camembert

Nothing is as smooth, creamy and wonderful as warmed Camembert unless it is warmed Camembert with almonds and butter.

*small whole Camembert (4¹/₂ ounces), room temperature*
*baking spray or butter*
1  *Tablespoon sliced almonds*
1  *teaspoon butter, chilled and sliced thinly*
   *sliced French bread*

Preheat broiler.

Slice the top crust off the cheese. (This is easier to do when the cheese is chilled.)

Spray a cookie sheet with baking spray (or grease it lightly) and place cheese on it, cut side up. Top with almonds, then cover the almonds with thin slices of butter.

Broil the cheese about 6 inches from the heat for 3 to 5 minutes. Watch it carefully. When the almonds are pale gold and the cheese looks a little oozy, it is ready. Use a wide spatula to lift the cheese carefully onto a serving plate. Surround the cheese with sliced French bread and provide small knives for spreading.

**Note:** You can do the same thing for large parties with a bigger wheel of Camembert or Brie. In this case, set it on the baking sheet on a piece of greased foil. To lift it, use two spatulas, and hold your breath.

**Yield:** 2 to 6 servings

---

Quick Tip
Most broiled things brown very quickly. Once you slip them under the broiler, don't get involved in something else.

---

# Smoked Oyster Cheese Dip

Smooth, rich, smoky and cheesy, this dip is worth fighting over.

    *1   can (3¹/₂ to 4 ounces) smoked oysters*
    *8   ounces smoked Cheddar or Gouda cheese, cubed*
    *1   package (8 ounces) cream cheese, cubed*
  *¹/₄  cup sour cream*
  *¹/₄  teaspoon Dijon mustard*
  *¹/₄  cup half and half, or to taste*

Crush the smoked oysters with a fork and put them in a heavy, medium-sized saucepan along with the cubed cheeses and sour cream. Heat slowly over low heat until the cheeses are melted. Stir in mustard. If the mixture is too thick for easy dipping, add enough half and half to make it a good dipping consistency.

Serve with toasted French bread, good melba toast or any warmed, crisp crackers.

**Yield:** about 2½ cups

# Southwestern Chili Dip

A marvelous hot chili made wickedly rich with cream cheese.

   1   *can (10 ounces) chili without beans*
   1   *can (4 ounces) chopped green chilies, drained*
   1   *package (8 ounces) cream cheese*
   1   *Tablespoon chili powder (or more to taste)*
   1   *can (4 ounces) chopped black olives*

In a medium saucepan, heat chili to the boiling point. Stir in drained green chilies, cream cheese, chili powder and olives. Heat gently, stirring until the cheese is melted and all is well blended.

Serve hot in a chafing dish or a serving bowl placed over a warmer, accompanied by tortilla chips.

**Yield:** 8 servings

# Cheesy Crab Dip

This dip can be made in seconds and it is creamy and rich tasting.

   1   *jar (8 ounces) processed cheese spread*
   1   *package (8 ounces) cream cheese*
   1   *cup crab, well picked over for cartilage*

In medium saucepan or chafing dish over medium-low heat, heat cheeses until melted, stirring frequently. Add crab and continue to heat until bubbly.

Serve hot in a chafing dish or over a warmer. Delicious with chunks of warmed French bread, corn or potato chips or toasted pita wedges.

**Yield:** 3 cups

---

**The Quick Cook** 🕐

Substitute 1 can (7 1/2) ounces crab, well rinsed and drained, for the fresh crab meat.

---

# Neapolitan Fondue

A zesty Italian tomato-beef-cheese combination, perfect for a cold winter night. It's a good dish for teenagers, but don't discount the adults. This is the sort of thing you end up eating with spoons.

| | |
|---|---|
| 8 | *ounces ground beef* |
| *1/2* | *envelope (1 1/2 ounce size) dry spaghetti sauce mix* |
| 1 | *can (15 ounces) tomato sauce* |
| 12 | *ounces (3 cups) Cheddar cheese, shredded* |
| 4 | *ounces ( 1 cup) mozzarella cheese, shredded* |
| 1 | *Tablespoon cornstarch* |
| *1/2* | *cup red wine* |
| | *crisp crusted Italian bread, cut in bite-size pieces or toasted pita bread wedges* |

In a heavy saucepan over medium high heat, brown meat and drain off the fat. Stir in spaghetti sauce mix and tomato sauce. Gradually add the cheeses. Stir over low heat until cheese is melted.

In a small bowl mix cornstarch and wine. Add to the cheese mixture. Continue to heat and stir until it is thickened and bubbly. Don't be alarmed if the cheese seems to get stringy at first — the wine does this; it will smooth out as it heats.

Serve hot in a chafing dish, a fondue pot, or any container that can sit over a warmer. Accompany it with bread cubes. If you serve this fondue-style, provide forks on which to impale the bread and swizzle it around in the sauce. If you want to treat it as a "dip", cut the bread in slices or sticks.

**Yield:** 10 to 12 servings

# Cold Pickups

◆

## Turkey-Roquefort Rolls

These are elegant. Roquefort cheese makes a lovely contrast to the mild turkey. Of course, you can substitute any veined cheese such as blue or Gorgonzola. The taste will be different with each, but they're all delicious.

> 8   ounces Roquefort cheese, room temperature
> 8   ounces cream cheese, room temperature
> $^1/_4$   cup sour cream
> 1   Tablespoon Worcestershire sauce
> 1   small clove garlic, minced
>      salt, to taste
> 8   thin slices turkey breast

In a small bowl mix Roquefort, cream cheese, sour cream, Worcestershire sauce and garlic. Taste and add salt if needed; the Roquefort will probably make it salty enough.

Spread the mixture on the turkey slices and roll up starting at the narrow side. Cut in 1-inch lengths.

**Note:** The rolls cut more easily if chilled. Thirty minutes in the refrigerator is standard chilling time, but I find that 10 minutes in the freezer does just about as well. If you have no time to chill, just cut gently.

**Yield:** 16 to 24

# Ham-Liverwurst Rolls

Ham and liverwurst or pâté is a classic French combination, and when you taste these little rolls you will see why. Should you have some real pâté languishing in the refrigerator, by all means substitute it for the liverwurst — either way the recipe is wonderful.

  4 ounces best quality liverwurst
  5 teaspoons butter, room temperature
  1 Tablespoon chives, chopped
  2 teaspoons parsley, chopped
1½ Tablespoons sherry
  ⅛ teaspoon cracked black peppercorns
  8 thin slices ham

Using a hand mixer, food processor or blender, mix liverwurst, butter, chives, parsley, sherry and peppercorns until fluffy. Spread the mixture on the ham slices, roll them up and cut in 1-inch lengths.

**Note:** The rolls cut more easily if chilled. Thirty minutes in the refrigerator is standard chilling time, but I find that 10 minutes in the freezer does just about as well. If you haven't time to chill, just cut very gently.

**Yield:** 20 to 24

---

**Quick Tip** 
Review your recipe in advance. If it calls for ingredients such as cream cheese or butter to be at room temperature, remove those items from the refrigerator in the morning so they'll be ready when you begin cooking.

# Smoked Salmon-Asparagus Rolls

We first ate this delicacy at a posh Watergate party. My greed must have shown because when we approached the elevator to leave, the waiter came over and offered us a few for the road. A word of advice: these are for high-living, no-compromise days. Inexpensive ingredients will embarrass you and bore your guests whereas the best salmon and fat, freshly cooked asparagus will produce pure heaven.

3   *Tablespoons Dijon mustard*
3   *Tablespoons sugar*
1   *Tablespoon vinegar*
3   *Tablespoons vegetable oil*
$1/4$   *teaspoon salt, or to taste*
10   *spears freshly cooked asparagus*
4   *ounces smoked salmon, thinly sliced*

In a small bowl whisk together mustard, sugar, vinegar, vegetable oil and salt. Pour in a small serving bowl and set aside.

Use only the tips of the asparagus, making them about 3 inches long. Wrap each in a 2-inch wide slice of salmon. You won't need to secure with a toothpick; it will adhere to itself.

Serve cold with the mustard sauce for dipping. Provide napkins because this is finger food.

**Yield:** 10

# Beef and Brie Croissants

A few words of advice: the roast beef must be of the best quality and thinly sliced and small croissants are better than big ones. (Filling quantities are for the frozen croissants that come four to a 6-ounce package.) That said, prepare for a treat.

    4   fresh or frozen croissants
    4   ounces roast beef, thinly sliced, room temperature
    2   ounces Brie cheese, room temperature

Heat croissants as directed on package or place fresh croissants in a 325° oven until warmed through. With a sharp knife slice in half as for a sandwich. On each croissant bottom place a fourth of the roast beef and ¼-inch thick slices of Brie to cover the length of the croissant — it won't cover the width, but you don't want it to. Put on the top of croissant.

Cut each sandwich into fourths and spear each section with a toothpick. It's easiest to make your cuts mentally, put in the picks, and then do the actual cutting.

Serve at room temperature, or best of all, ever so slightly warmed.
**Yield:** 16

---

# Daniel's Roquefort Endive

A sophisticated combination. Tangy cheese, fresh endive, and walnuts put smooth, crisp and crunch into one bite.

     3      ounces Roquefort cheese, room temperature
     3      ounces cream cheese, room temperature
25 to 30   walnut halves
25 to 30   Belgian endive leaves

In a bowl mash the cheese until well blended. Place a small mound of cheese mixture on the thick end of each endive leaf. Top the cheese with a walnut half. Transfer to a platter and serve at room temperature.
**Yield:** 25 to 30

# Shrimp Roquefort Splits

Oooh are these good!

    6   *ounces Roquefort cheese, room temperature*
  12   *cooked jumbo shrimp, peeled and deveined*

In a small bowl cream the cheese to make it easy to shape.

Halve each shrimp lengthwise and place 1 tablespoon of cheese between the two halves of shrimp. Spear each shrimp with a cocktail pick and serve at room temperature, feeling terribly rich and pampered.

**Yield:** 12

# Artichoke-Shrimp Canapés

Very elegant, very pretty. The shrimp must be small or the canapé will be the sort that requires a jaw that unhinges.

      24   *slices French bread, ¼-inch thick, 2 inches in diameter*
       1   *cup tartar sauce (approximately)*
12 to 15   *canned artichoke hearts (in water pack)*
       1   *pound small shrimp, cooked, shelled and deveined*
          *salt, to taste*
          *freshly ground pepper, to taste*
      24   *strips pimento*

Toast the French bread lightly. Spread each slice with a generous half teaspoon of tartar sauce. Cut artichoke hearts in ½-inch slices. Place a slice on each toast and top with a shrimp. Sprinkle lightly with salt, grind on a little pepper, then add a small bit of tartar sauce and a strip of pimento.

Check the solidity of your structure and if it seems teetery, secure by spearing straight down with a toothpick.

**Yield:** 24

# Mimosa Shrimp

Chilled shrimps bathed in a marvelous vinaigrette sauce.

6 *Tablespoons olive oil*
6 *Tablespoons vegetable oil*
1 *Tablespoon dijon mustard*
$1/4$ *teaspoon salt*
$1/8$ *teaspoon paprika*
1 *hard-cooked egg, coarsely chopped*
$1/4$ *cup coarsely chopped celery*
$1/4$ *cup coarsely chopped green pepper*
1 *Tablespoon grated onion*
1 *Tablespoon chopped parsley*
2 *cups (approximately 1 to 1$1/2$ pounds) medium to large cooked shrimp, peeled and deveined*

In a food processor container or blender place olive oil, vegetable oil, mustard, salt and paprika. Blend on low speed until you have a thick emulsion. Turn the motor off and add egg, celery, green pepper, onion and parsley. Blend for 5 seconds only. You want these last ingredients to be chopped, not pureed.

Place the cooked shrimp in a shallow serving bowl. Pour the sauce over the mix lightly to ensure that each shrimp is well coated. Serve with toothpicks or on small plates with forks.

**Yield:** 8 servings

# Oriental Turkey or Chicken Cubes

The turkey chunks are dipped first in a lovely Oriental mayonnaise, then in nuts — it's quick, cold, and crunchy.

1 *pound cooked turkey or chicken meat in a large chunk*
1 *cup mayonnaise*
1 *teaspoon soy sauce*
1 *teaspoon grated fresh ginger root*
1 *cup (approximately) blanched, toasted almonds, chopped*

Cut turkey or chicken into 1-inch cubes and place on a serving plate. In a small bowl, mix mayonnaise, soy sauce and ginger root.

Serve meat cubes accompanied by a bowl of sauce and a bowl of chopped almonds. Provide toothpicks. Guests should spear a piece of cooked chicken or turkey, dunk it in sauce, then in the nuts.

If you are in a nurturing mood and want to do the whole thing yourself, roll the cubes in sauce, then in nuts, spear them and place, ready-to-eat, on a platter.

**Note:** To toast almonds, spread them on baking sheet in one layer. Bake at 300° for 8 to 12 minutes. Watch carefully.

**Yield:** 8 servings

# Sun-Dried Tomatoes, Basil and Cheese ⏰

Serve this when you want to clinch your reputation as someone who knows food. It is sophisticated and delicious. What's more, it falls into the flash category.

|          |                                                    |
|---------:|----------------------------------------------------|
|          | *crackers or toast rounds*                         |
| 6 to 8   | *ounces goat cheese (chèvre) or cream cheese*      |
|          | *olive oil*                                        |
|          | *coarsely ground pepper*                           |
| 18 to 24 | *fresh basil leaves (if very large, use halves)*   |
| 1        | *bottle (10 to 12 ounces) sun-dried tomatoes in oil* |

On a cracker or toast round, place a piece of cheese about ¼-inch thick. Drizzle with a drop or two of olive oil, grind on a little pepper, lay on a fresh basil leaf and top with a sun-dried tomato. If the tomatoes are large, cut them in half.

Of course, you can make up a plate of these yourself, but why not set out the makings and let your guests assemble their own? If you do, find a pretty cruet for the olive oil. And provide a pepper mill, of course.

**Yield:** 18 to 24

# Roast Beef-Horseradish Roulades

These seem to appeal to the macho in men — but even non-liberated women have been known to eat inordinate amounts.

|       |                                                  |
|------:|--------------------------------------------------|
| 1 | *package (8 ounces) cream cheese, room temperature* |
| ¹/₄ to ¹/₃ | *cup sour cream* |
| 1 to 4 | *Tablespoons prepared horseradish* |
| 1 | *Tablespoon fresh lemon juice* |
|   | *salt and pepper, to taste* |
| 16 to 18 | *thin slices rare roast beef* |

In a small bowl cream the cheese with enough sour cream to make it spread easily. Add horseradish, lemon juice, salt and pepper. Taste and add more horseradish or lemon as needed to make a nippy filling. Spread cheese mixture about ¼-inch thick on beef slices. Roll up. Fasten with a toothpick if necessary. Serve cold.

**Note:** If the rolls are very long, cut them in half. They slice more easily when chilled. Thirty minutes in the refrigerator is standard chilling time, but I find that 10 minutes in the freezer does just about as well. If there's no time to chill, just cut very gently.

**Yield:** 16 to 18

# Radish Canapés

Pretty, fresh and crunchy. These make a delightful contrast to any hors d'oeuvres assortment.

16 radishes, washed and trimmed of stems and roots
2 Tablespoons butter, room temperature
6 ounces cream cheese, room temperature
1 Tablespoon chopped parsley
1 teaspoon chopped chives
3 teaspoons lemon juice
salt, to taste
freshly ground pepper, to taste
6 slices pumpernickel, rye, or firm-textured white bread

Grate radishes in a food processor or by hand. Place them in a towel and squeeze out extra moisture.

In a medium bowl cream butter and cheese until fluffy. Add parsley, chives, lemon juice, salt and pepper and half the radishes. Spread this mixture on the bread and cut each slice into 4 or 6 pieces. Top each generously with the remaining radishes.

Serve cool or at room temperature.

**Yield:** 24 to 36, depending on how you cut the bread

# Doo Hickey (Radishes and Cheese)

Both the Scandinavians and the French eat radishes as hors d'oeuvres, either with butter or cheese. This combination, using Swiss cheese, is especially fresh-tasting.

28   medium radishes
2 to 3   ounces Swiss cheese slices

Clean radishes and cut off the stems and leaves. Make a cut in each, cutting down from the top. Cut down again at an angle to the first cut to remove a very narrow wedge-shaped piece. Cut cheese into 1-inch squares. Insert a piece of cheese into each radish.

Serve cold. Wonderful with cold beer or a martini.

**Yield:** 28

# Ellen's Cucumber Sandwiches

Cucumber sandwiches have an undeserved reputation as effete, curled-pinkie food. But they're so wonderful. Try my friend Ellen's version with their little caviar knobs, or omit the caviar and savor the crispness of cucumber and mayonnaise.

6 to 8   slices of firm-textured white bread
   ¹/₂   cup mayonnaise
     24   slices peeled cucumber, about ¹/₄-inch thick
       2   ounces caviar, black or red

Cut the bread into 24 rounds, the same diameter as the cucumber. Spread the bread rounds generously with mayonnaise. Top each round with a cucumber slice. Dot the tops with mayonnaise. Don't be stingy with the mayo when you make these; it's what gives the wonderful contrast. Using a small spoon, top each canapé with a tiny mound of caviar.

Serve the sandwiches chilled or at room temperature.

**Yield:** 24

# Pecan Mushrooms

These cold stuffed mushrooms are a fascinating combination of flavors and textures. They offer a wonderful contrast to most cocktail food.

    2  Tablespoons butter
    1  Tablespoon Worcestershire sauce
    24 large pecan halves, left whole or coarsely chopped
    24 medium-size mushrooms
    4  ounces cream cheese (¹/₂ cup)

In a medium skillet, melt butter and add Worcestershire sauce. When the mixture bubbles, add the nuts and stir over medium heat until they are well coated. Drain on paper towels.

Wipe mushrooms with a damp cloth. Carefully pull out the stems and save them for another use. Fill each mushroom cap with about a teaspoon of cream cheese. Top with a pecan half or pat on a good coating of chopped pecans.

**Note:** Whether you chop the pecans or not depends on their size and the size of the mushrooms. What you want is to cover all of the cheese with nuts. If you have fat pecan halves and smallish mushrooms, leave the nuts whole; if an entire half won't do the job, chop them up.

**Variation:** The sautéed pecans make a great snack by themselves. Try doubling the pecan portion of the recipe and serve the nuts in a pretty bowl.

**Yield:** 24

# Cold Dips
# & Dunks

◆

## Louisiana Whipped Chili Dip

A real treasure from the Bayou country. The sauce is suave and delicate and utterly seductive; delicious with seafood, chicken or marinated artichoke hearts. You will probably find a thousand uses for it. I have. (P.S. Don't let the amount of sugar put you off. That's what gives this dip the wonderful, soft taste.)

> 1  cup whipping cream
> 1  cup mayonnaise
> 1  cup chili sauce
> 6  Tablespoons sugar
>    salt, to taste
>    hot pepper sauce, to taste

In a medium bowl whip the cream until stiff. Fold in mayonnaise, chili sauce, sugar, salt and hot pepper sauce to taste. Pour in a serving bowl.

Serve cold or at room temperature as a dip.

**Yield:** 2 cups

# Orange-Mustard Dip ⏰

This is a dip that improves almost everything you can think of. Try it with fried shrimp, sausages, chicken wings, ham chunks, etc.

- 1 cup orange marmalade
- 6 Tablespoons bottled horseradish
- 3 teaspoons Dijon mustard
- 3 teaspoons yellow mustard
- 4 teaspoons fresh lime juice
- 4 teaspoons port wine (or sherry or cognac)
- 1/2 teaspoon salt
- 1/4 teaspoon white pepper
- 2 teaspoons paprika

Into a blender jar or food processor bowl put marmalade, horseradish, mustards, lime juice, port wine, salt, pepper and paprika. Blend or process until smooth; no more than 5 to 8 seconds. Pour into a serving bowl.

Serve as a dip with fried shrimp or chicken, or any other foods you want to adorn. Like basic black, it goes with just about everything.

**Yield:** about 1½ cups

# Snowy Chili Cheese Dip

This is fresh and snappy and different. The fiery jalapeños make a delicious contrast to the cool, bland cheese. This recipe serves less than you think because it is so light.

> 2   cups (1 pint) large-curd creamed cottage cheese
> ½   cup canned tomatoes flavored with green chilies
>     (available in the Mexican section of your grocery)
> 3   Tablespoons jalapeño peppers, chopped coarsely
> 1   teaspoon salt
> 1   avocado, in small chunks

In a medium bowl mix cottage cheese, tomato-chili mixture, jalapeño peppers, salt and avocado. Taste and add more chilies if you like.

Serve cold with corn chips or crisp crackers.

**Variation:** Substitute ½ cup jalapeño relish for the tomatoes with chilis and chopped jalapeños.

**Yield:** about 3 cups

# Pimento Dip 🕰

Creamy, piquant and a lovely deep orange color. I especially like this with corn-based dippers. It is also good with vegetables, but be sure to cut them thin so the pimento gets a chance to assert itself.

> 1   jar (7 ounces) whole pimento, drained
> 8   ounces cream cheese, room temperature
>     salt, to taste
> ½   teaspoon hot sauce (or to taste)

In a blender or food processor, place drained pimento and cream cheese and blend thoroughly. Add salt and hot sauce to taste. Place in bowl and serve with corn chips or raw vegetables.

**Yield:** about 2 cups

# Jalapeño-Tuna Dip

My husband eats this with a spoon. It's delicious. Do make an effort to find the fresh cilantro (coriander) because it makes the dish, although people have been known to eat it enthusiastically when topped with a parsley substitute.

1   jar or can (6 ounces) jalapeño peppers, whole or sliced
2   cans (7 ounces each) tuna, drained
³/₄   cup minced onion
¹/₂   cup mayonnaise
¹/₄ to ¹/₂   cup chopped cilantro (fresh coriander)

Chop the peppers coarsely and save the liquid. In a large bowl mix tuna, peppers and their liquid, mashing down well with fork. You want to achieve the texture of tuna salad. Add onions and enough mayonnaise to make a good dipping consistency.

Place in a serving bowl and sprinkle generously with chopped cilantro. Serve with any sort of chips or crackers.

**Yield:** about 4 cups

# Curry Cream Dip

Wonderful for fresh vegetables.

¹/₂   cup mayonnaise
¹/₂   cup sour cream
1   Tablespoon sugar
1   teaspoon garlic salt
1   teaspoon curry powder
1   teaspoon prepared horseradish
1   teaspoon grated onion
1   Tablespoon vinegar

In a medium bowl mix all ingredients. Serve cold surrounded by fresh vegetables for dipping.

**Yield:** 1 cup

# Sesame Dip

This recipe comes from a Middle Eastern friend. The toasted sesame seeds give an exotic tang of both Middle East and Orient. We love it with toasted pita wedges, French bread or raw vegetables.

3   *Tablespoons sesame seeds*
3   *Tablespoons peanut oil*
1   *Tablespoon white vinegar*
1   *Tablespoon soy sauce*
$1/2$   *cup whipping cream*
$1/4$   *teaspoon garlic salt*
    *salt, to taste*
3   *grinds pepper*

In a dry, heavy skillet over medium-high heat, roast sesame seeds for 1 to 2 minutes, or until they turn a pale gold. Be careful; they brown suddenly and are bitter if they burn.

Put toasted seeds in a blender with the oil, vinegar and soy sauce. Blend until smooth. In a small bowl whip the cream to soft peaks and fold in the blended mixture. Taste and season with garlic salt, salt and pepper.

Serve with pita wedges, any chips, French bread or raw vegetables.

**Yield:** about 1½ cups

# Tostada Dip

So many wonderful contrasts in one dip. This is a perennial favorite.

*½ cup sour cream*
*¼ cup mayonnaise*
*1 package (1¼ ounces) taco seasoning mix*
*3 large avocados*
*3 Tablespoons lemon juice*
*1½ cans (10-ounce size) bean dip*
*1 bunch spring onions, chopped (include all the green)*
*1 large tomato, diced*
*1 can (4 ounces) chopped black olives*
*1 can (4 ounces) chopped green chilies, drained*
*2 hard-cooked eggs, chopped*
*1 cup Monterey Jack cheese, shredded*
*1 cup sharp Cheddar cheese, shredded*

In a small bowl mix sour cream, mayonnaise and taco seasoning. In another bowl mash avocados and mix with the lemon juice. On a shallow dish or serving platter (about 9-inches x 13-inches) spread the bean dip. Top it with the sour cream mixture, spreading to cover. Then cover with the mashed avocado. Layer on the following in order, using all of each item: spring onions, tomato, olives, green chilies, eggs, Monterey Jack cheese, and for the final layer, the Cheddar cheese.

Serve at room temperature with large tortilla chips for dipping.

**Yield:** 12 servings

# Zucchini Rémoulade

A wonderful, fresh-tasting combination of julienned zucchini and mustardy mayonnaise. Scoop it up on chips or eat as a fork hors d'oeuvre.

   1½   *pounds zucchini (about 8 small ones)*
   ¾    *cup mayonnaise*
   1    *Tablespoon Dijon mustard*
   1    *Tablespoon chopped parsley*
   1    *Tablespoon capers, drained and chopped*
   ½    *teaspoon salt*
   ¼    *teaspoon dried tarragon*

In a food processor using the medium grater or the julienne disk, cut zucchini in julienne. If you don't have a food processor, cut it by hand as follows: cut each zucchini in ¼-inch slices, stack the slices and cut them into ¼-inch wide matchsticks.

Squeeze the zucchini in a towel to remove some of the moisture, then place it in a bowl along with the mayonnaise, mustard, parsley, capers, salt and tarragon. Toss until everything is well mixed. Taste and correct the seasoning if necessary.

Heap the mixture in a pretty serving bowl and surround it with corn or potato chips, toasted pita wedges or French bread. Or provide small plates and forks.

**Yield:** 4 to 5 cups

# Sue's Spinach Dip

This is a delicious recipe to have in your arsenal.

    2   packages (10 ounces each) frozen chopped spinach
    3/4 package dry leek soup mix, about 1/2 cup
    1/2 cup chopped parsley
    1/2 cup chopped spring onions
    1   cup sour cream
    1   cup mayonnaise
    1/3 cup grated parmesan cheese
        salt, to taste
        freshly ground black pepper, to taste

Cook spinach as directed on package and drain well, pressing out all the water. Place in food processor bowl or blender with the soup mix, parsley, spring onions, sour cream, mayonnaise, and parmesan cheese. Process lightly to combine well. Add salt and pepper to taste and pour into a pretty serving bowl. As with any dip, chilling will ripen the flavor.

Serve with potato chips, tortilla chips or with toasted pita wedges.

Yield: 3 to 3½ cups

# Judy's Hummos

A garlicky puree of chick peas from the Middle East. This is how my friend Judy, who has spent years in that region, taught me to make it.

|         |                                                          |
|---------|----------------------------------------------------------|
| 1       | *can (16 to 20 ounces) chick peas, drained (reserve liquid)* |
| 2       | *large cloves garlic, peeled*                            |
| 3 to 4  | *Tablespoons lemon juice*                                |
| 2       | *Tablespoons tahini*                                     |
| 1 to 2  | *teaspoons salt*                                         |
| 4 to 5  | *grinds pepper*                                          |
|         | *reserved chick pea liquid*                              |
|         | *minced parsley, for garnish*                            |

In food processor bowl or blender jar, put drained chick peas, garlic, 3 tablespoons of lemon juice, tahini, 1 teaspoon salt and pepper. Add 2 to 3 tablespoons of the reserved chick pea liquid. Puree for about 30 seconds, scrape down the bowl, and puree again, adding a little more chick pea liquid if necessary to achieve a puree that is soft but still thick enough to hold its shape on a spoon. Taste for seasoning and add more lemon juice and salt, if needed. (Lemons vary so in tartness that it is impossible to give a specific amount.)

Place hummos in a pretty bowl and garnish with parsley. Serve with pita wedges (fresh or toasted).

**Note:** Tahini is sesame seed paste and is available at many supermarkets, all health food and Middle Eastern food shops.

**Yield:** 2 cups

# Layered Caviar Dip

A favorite of my friend Margaret who entertains often and elegantly and who knows good food.

> 5   hard-cooked eggs
> 2   spring onions
> 1½  cups sour cream
> 2   jars (4 ounces each) black caviar
>     juice of 1 lemon
>     melba toast

Use a pretty glass serving dish that holds about 6 cups and is about 8 inches in diameter. If the layering can show through the glass, so much the better.

Chop the eggs quite finely. Chop the spring onions finely using part of the green. Place the eggs in the serving bowl. Top them with the onions, distributing them evenly. Layer on the sour cream, spreading to cover. Carefully spoon the caviar on the sour cream layer, distributing evenly. Squeeze the lemon juice over all.

Serve chilled or at room temperature with melba toast squares.

**Note:** Look for little 2-inch square toasts about ¼ to ½-inch thick. Their texture is a bit like a rusk, and they are wonderful with this.

**Yield:** 6 to 8 servings

---

**Quick Tip** 🕐
Boiled eggs are sometimes available at the deli, so check yours. If you know ahead that you'll be entertaining, boil eggs a day or so ahead. Or, boil them in the morning while you're drinking coffee.

# Cold Spreads

◆

## Strawberry Cheese-Nut Ring

Don't shake your head and pass this one up. It sounds implausible, but remember how good strawberry preserves taste with cheese soufflé. This is the same combination of contrasting sweet, salty, fruity and suave.

|  |  |
|---|---|
| 1 | pound medium sharp or sharp Cheddar, grated |
| 1 | cup finely chopped walnuts, divided |
| 1 | cup mayonnaise |
| $^1/_3$ | cup minced onion |
| 3 to 4 | grinds of black pepper |
| $^1/_2$ to 1 | teaspoon cayenne pepper |
| 1 | cup (or more) strawberry preserves |

In a medium bowl mix cheese, half the walnuts, all the mayonnaise and onion. Add black pepper and cayenne pepper to taste. Put the mixture on a round serving plate, shaping it into a rather flat-topped mound about 2 to 3 inches high. Make a depression in the center that will hold about ¾ cup. Spoon the preserves into this well. Press the reserved nuts around the edge.

Serve with a small bowl of extra preserves. Provide knives for spreading and plenty of crisp crackers, melba toast or pumernickel bread.

**Note:** You'll be amazed at the amount of strawberry preserves used. You might want to have an extra cup available for refilling.

**Yield:** about 4 cups

# Two Minute Elegant Pâté ⏰

This tastes like the expensive French pâté de foie gras — rich, luscious and heavenly. You can serve it with pride to your most discerning friends.

> 1   cup butter, slightly softened
> 1   can (4 ounces) liver pâté
> 2 to 3   grinds of black pepper
> 2   Tablespoons brandy

Using an electric mixer or food processor, cream butter until fluffy. Beat in pâté, pepper and brandy. Chill if you have time. If not, just put it in pretty bowl and serve with French or Italian bread or with melba toast.

Yield: 6 to 8 servings

---

# Caviar Quickie ⏰

For the toast use high quality, firm-textured bread, not the floppy stuff kids like for peanut butter sandwiches.

> 12   hot toast rounds, well buttered (3 to 4 slices bread)
> 1   jar (4 ounces) caviar, chilled
> 1/2   cup sour cream, chilled

Set out all ingredients: toast, hot and buttery; caviar and sour cream, chilled. Put small, silver spoons in the caviar and cream.

Guests top the toast first with caviar, then with a little sour cream. This is the time when, if you own tiny cloth napkins, you might set them out.

**Variation:** Some people would add small bowls of chopped onion and hard cooked egg, yolk and whites minced and served separately. Purists would object. I wouldn't really. And it might make the caviar go farther.

**Yield:** 6 servings